Facts About the Panther

By Lisa Strattin

© 2019 Lisa Strattin

Revised 2022 © Lisa Strattin

FREE BOOK

FREE FOR ALL SUBSCRIBERS

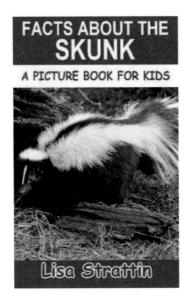

LisaStrattin.com/Subscribe-Here

BOX SET

- **FACTS ABOUT THE POISON DART FROGS**
- **FACTS ABOUT THE THREE TOED SLOTH**
- **FACTS ABOUT THE RED PANDA**
- **FACTS ABOUT THE SEAHORSE**
- **FACTS ABOUT THE PLATYPUS**
- **FACTS ABOUT THE REINDEER**
- **FACTS ABOUT THE PANTHER**
- **FACTS ABOUT THE SIBERIAN HUSKY**

LisaStrattin.com/BookBundle

Facts for Kids Picture Books by Lisa Strattin

Little Blue Penguin, Vol 92

Chipmunk, Vol 5

Frilled Lizard, Vol 39

Blue and Gold Macaw, Vol 13

Poison Dart Frogs, Vol 50

Blue Tarantula, Vol 115

African Elephants, Vol 8

Amur Leopard, Vol 89

Sabre Tooth Tiger, Vol 167

Baboon, Vol 174

Sign Up for New Release Emails Here

LisaStrattin.com/subscribe-here

★★COVER IMAGE★★

https://www.flickr.com/photos/scottmliddell/4599259438/

★★ADDITIONAL IMAGES★★

https://www.flickr.com/photos/berniedup/51833621634/

https://www.flickr.com/photos/bensonkua/14581961874/

https://www.flickr.com/photos/barrasa8/4635644323/

https://www.flickr.com/photos/30478819@N08/25242396338/

https://www.flickr.com/photos/150792268@N02/37618848516/

https://www.flickr.com/photos/e3000/6790044660/

https://www.flickr.com/photos/johnshortland/6159758831/

https://www.flickr.com/photos/47847725@N04/4530714641/

https://www.flickr.com/photos/pokerbrit/10037053435/

https://www.flickr.com/photos/hisgett/4375024092/

Contents

INTRODUCTION

The Panther (also commonly known as the Black Panther) is a large member of the Big Cat family, native to Asia, Africa, and the Americas. The Panther is not a distinct species itself but is the general name used to refer to any black colored feline of the Big Cat family, most notably Leopards and Jaguars.

The Panther is an elusive and powerful animal that has adapted well to a variety of habitats around the world and is known to be one of the strongest climbers of all felines. Although the Panther is not technically classified as a separate species, they are considered to be endangered by many due to the declining numbers of both Leopards and Jaguars throughout much of their natural ranges.

CHARACTERISTICS

The Panther is an incredibly intelligent and agile animal that is seldom seen by people in the wild because they are quiet and cautious animals. Their dark brown, almost black, fur camouflages the panther both into the surrounding forest and makes them almost invisible in the darkness of night. It is a solitary animal that leads a nocturnal lifestyle, spending much of the daylight hours resting safely high in trees. Like both the leopard and the jaguar, panthers are incredible climbers and they not only rest in the trees, but they are also able to keep a watchful eye out for prey without being spotted. It is an incredibly powerful and fearless animal that is feared by many due to the fact that they are aggressive. The panther is very territorial, particularly males, whose home ranges overlap those of a number of females.

Although technically black leopards and jaguars are considered to be the only true panthers by science, the term is also used to describe a number of other dark coated cats in their native habitats. The black panther is seen to be one of the most intelligent and ferocious predators in America, so the image of a panther is widely used as a logo or as a mascot for sports teams. Some are able to swim, as some are known to have a real love of water. Not only do these individuals prefer flooded forests but they spend a remarkable amount of time swimming, playing, and hunting in the cooling water.

APPEARANCE

The Panther tends to be dark brown to black in color and is otherwise identical to other feline species. The only real exception to this is the Florida Panther found in the south east region of the USA, that is believed to be a subspecies of Cougar and is quite rarely dark brown in color and tends to have more of a speckled appearance. The panther has no spots on its long body or tail, but instead has a shiny coat of dark fur. They have small heads with strong jaws and emerald green eyes and tend to have hind legs that are larger and slightly longer than those at the front.

LIFE STAGES

Although there are only two different species of Big Cat considered to be Panthers, Leopards and Jaguars are actually very closely related despite living in separate parts of the world. Black Leopards and Jaguars often are born in the same litter as spotted cubs with the female giving birth to between 2 and 4 cubs after a gestation period of around 3 months. It is a simple recessive gene carried by both parents that makes a cub black. Panther cubs are born blind and do not open their eyes until they are nearly two weeks old.

They are incredibly vulnerable to predators, particularly when left by their mother who must hunt for their food. By the time they are a few months old, the cubs begin to accompany her in search of prey and often won't leave her until they are nearly 2 years old having established a territory for themselves.

LIFE SPAN

Panthers live on average between 12 to 15 years in the wild. The greatest risk to them is when they are young cubs and other animals can kill them.

SIZE

Panthers grow to be as long as 75 inches, which is just over 6 feet and can weigh as much as 350 pounds!

HABITAT

Panthers are natively found on three continents, with their location depending on whether or not it is a Black Leopard or a Black Jaguar. There are 30 different subspecies of Leopard found across both Asia and sub-Saharan Africa, and with the once large natural range of the Jaguar stretching throughout Central and South America and even into parts of the USA, the Panther has become an incredibly adaptable animal that is found in a variety of different habitats.

Although they are most commonly found in tropical and deciduous forests, the Panther can also be found inhabiting both marsh and swampland, along with grasslands and even more hostile areas such as deserts and mountains. Along with a number of the world's largest felines, it is becoming rarer in the wild primarily due to habitat loss in the form of deforestation.

DIET

The Panther is a carnivorous animal. Hunting under the cover of night, the big cat's dark fur makes it almost impossible to spot. This means that it can move through the jungle completely unseen by the prey it is hunting!

Although the majority of their hunting is actually done on the ground, they are also known to hunt from the trees; they can ambush their prey from above. The exact diet of the Panther depends on what is available where it lives in the world. Panthers will hunt deer, warthogs, wild boar, tapir, and antelope, as well as smaller game like birds and rabbits when larger prey is scarce.

ENEMIES

The panthers found in Africa and Asia are preyed upon by other large carnivores such as lions and hyenas, but the most common predator and biggest threat to them is people. Not only have these animals been hunted by people throughout much of their natural range, but they have also been subjected to drastic habitat loss due to deforestation for both expanding human settlements and to make way for agriculture. Population numbers of large Cats are declining all around the world and when they are being pushed into smaller and smaller pockets of their native habitats.

The world's big cats have been hunted by people for their fur and as trophy hunts. This has caused enormous declines in numbers of leopards and jaguars. Panthers have also been subjected to severe habitat degradation throughout much of Asia, Africa and America which means that these elusive predators are now even rarer.

They are very rarely seen by people who are only really ever aware of a Panther's presence by their tracks left on the ground and scratch marks on trees. They are in fact so sneaky that they are often referred to as 'the ghost of the forest.'

SUITABILITY AS PETS

It is obvious that the panther is not suitable as a pet.

Although there are select people who have an exotic pet license, in some areas, with the rights to own big cats. But for most of us, it's not a good choice!

COLOR ME

COLOR ME

COLOR ME

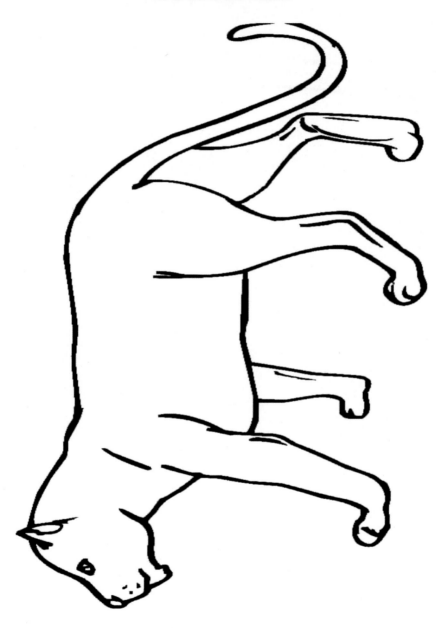

COLOR ME

COLOR ME

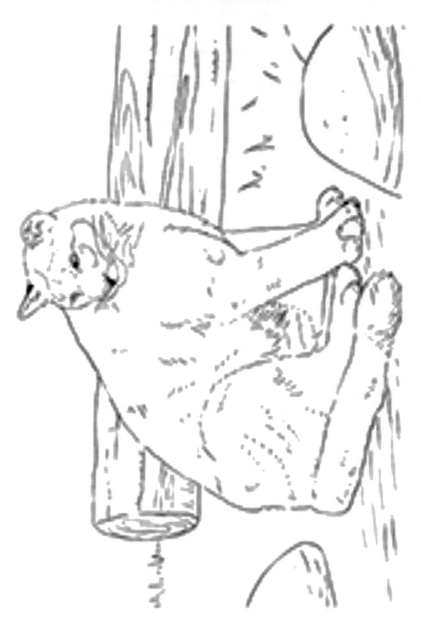

COLOR ME

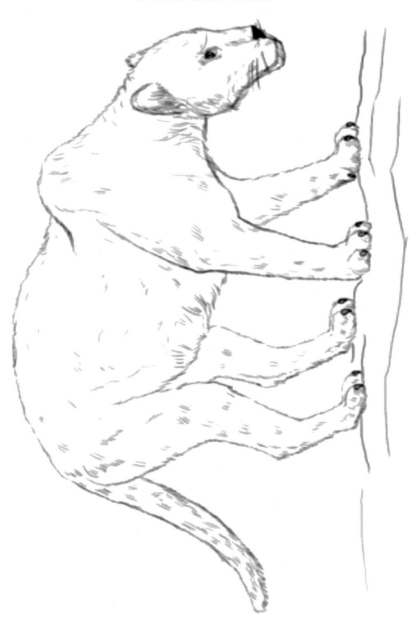

COLOR ME

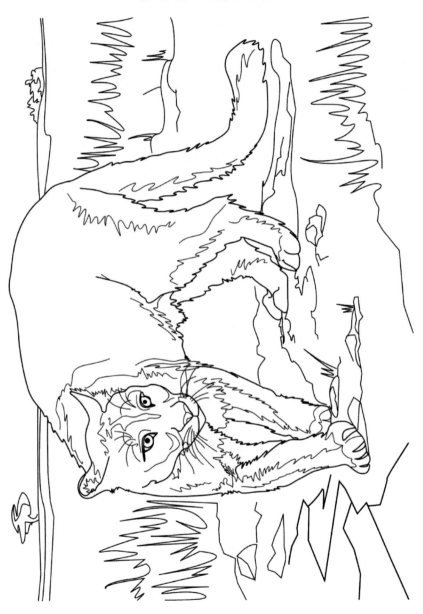

COLOR ME

COLOR ME

COLOR ME

Please leave me a review here:

LisaStrattin.com/Review-Vol-192

For more Kindle Downloads Visit Lisa Strattin Author Page on Amazon Author Central

amazon.com/author/lisastrattin

To see upcoming titles, visit my website at LisaStrattin.com– most books available on Kindle!

LisaStrattin.com

FREE BOOK

FOR ALL SUBSCRIBERS – SIGN UP NOW

LisaStrattin.com/Subscribe-Here

LisaStrattin.com/Facebook

LisaStrattin.com/Youtube

Made in the USA
Las Vegas, NV
04 March 2023

68531871R00026